Ballington Booth

The Soldier's Manual

Ballington Booth

The Soldier's Manual

ISBN/EAN: 9783337308681

Printed in Europe, USA, Canada, Australia, Japan

Cover: Foto ©ninafisch / pixelio.de

More available books at **www.hansebooks.com**

THE

SOLDIERS' MANUAL;

OR

PIETY AND PRACTICE.

NEW YORK.

PRINTED AND PUBLISHED AT THE SALVATION ARMY HEADQUARTERS,
111 READE STREET.

1889.

CONTENTS.

Godliness.

Practice.

THE

SOLDIERS' MANUAL.

Dear Comrades :—

For some time it has been on our hearts to place in your hands a small, plain book which would prove a help and guide to you in your warfare for God beneath the blood-and-fire flag of The Salvation Army. We do not propose, in the following pages, to enter into the doctrines, beliefs, measures, or rules, which guide and propel this great and God-inspired organization. All these subjects are entered into most fully and exhaustively in the six hundred and twenty-four pages of the F. O., as also in the " Orders and Regulations," and " Doctrines and Disciplines." We refer you to these books for all the information and instruction you may need concerning the Holy War. But in the following pages we propose to mention a number of the most essential points in a soldier's life and warfare, to be used for your own guidance, and we pray that you may read and re-read them and put them into practice if you have not done so already, that with the blessing of God this manual may succeed in leading you, and every comrade who shall enlist beneath the colors in this country, to be in every respect, in private life and public service, all that God and The Army calls for soldiers to be. As we write, and send forth into your midst these words of counsel, our hearts go out in sympathy and love for you in the trials and crosses of your warfare, and we want you more than ever to feel that we are ONE WITH YOU *in all that concerns the kingdom, and are living to prove ourselves ever your servants as well as your leaders in the Salvation War,*

BALLINGTON BOOTH,
MAUD B. BOOTH.

National Headquarters :
111 *Reade Street, New York City.*

THE SOLDIERS' MANUAL;

OR,

PIETY AND PRACTICE.

If there is a people on the face of the earth who are watched and criticised and talked about, above any other religious denomination, it is Salvationists. The eye of the world, as is natural, is far more ready to detect a fault or flaw in their profession, and far more ready to bring that which is inconsistent to light, using it as a weapon against us, than to notice the good points and good qualities of those who are professing enmity and renunciation for all that the world calls dear. We have to face this fact, and though it makes one of the crosses of our warfare, it should also

be one of our safeguards, as a constant reminder
of the importance of watching our every word
and deed and action.

Our profession is a very high one, and, the
higher the profession, the more conspicuous the
inconsistency of a life which does not correspond
with it. The whiter the garment, the more visible the stains or blotches; just so, dear comrade,
with a soul that has been washed white with the
blood of Jesus, the stains of some little fault,
allowed to mar its whiteness, will stand out
even more conspicuously than in the soul of one
who professes not to have known the cleansing
power of Calvary's stream. " Walk as children
of light."

The first and foremost necessity to the success-
fulness of the Salvationist's life is *piety—godliness.*

We don't believe in profession. We despise
talk, if it be *only* talk, and we believe that in
God's Army He only wants men and women
whose lives, in their every detail, are consistent
and true.

I.—GODLINESS IN PRIVATE.

There is a danger of not always living in the same spirit with which we rose from the penitent-form the night that we became recognized followers of the Man of Sorrows. How real Jesus seemed at that hour! How felt was His presence ! How ardent was that love that sang, " I will follow Thee, my Saviour," and what a longing and zeal for the welfare of the souls of men possessed our very being! The pages of the Bible that night seemed to have a new light shed on them, and whereas they were once tedious to read they then became almost an essential of life. Now we think that the same spirit and love and zeal should ever exist in the private heart-experience of every soldier, save that as years and months roll over them, it should become intensified and more and more part of their being. To maintain piety of heart and communion with God,

Ist. The soldier should separate himself from the world's sins and pleasures.

Do not allow your soul to be contaminated by

the influence of the world.   It is not only sin, folly and outward rebellion that God censures, but even the countenancing of it or association with it.   In the days of the children of Israel, not only was a dead body considered unclean, but the man and woman who touched it.   So, if you want to be pure, you must not touch or handle the unclean thing.   Some say that their associations are such that it is utterly impossible for them to cut loose from worldly practices and associations.   God's only answer is, that given in days of old to His people, "Choose ye this day whom ye will serve, God or Baal."   You must be out-and-out for God, or your soul piety will have but little chance of surviving longer than a few weeks.

"Be ye separate, saith the Lord, and touch not the unclean thing."

"Have no fellowship with the unfruitful works of darkness."

2d. The soldier must remember that his Bible is an essential to his spiritual growth and piety.

It is a very sure index that a man's soul is not where it ought to be if his Bible is laid by unmarked and unfingered, to be brought out only on a Sunday or on special occasions. Salvation soldiers should be Bible-lovers and Bible-readers. We do not mean in the sense in which many read it, simply as a sort of study, translating its prophecies by their own judgment or the judgment of others, or comparing and analyzing and explaining the inspired Word which, we hold, can only be rightly understood by an *inspired soul*. It must be read in the spirit. An officer once very truly said, "The Bible should be read in the light of the same lamp by which it was written."

You should read the Bible always remembering that you are but a little atom of dust compared to the great and mighty God who dictated it, and that it is your place to accept and believe His Word in the spirit, and that it is only thus that you can understand it, for it is impossible for the human mind to understand the Divine, unless it has been filled and inspired by the Divine Spirit.

Read your Bible *on your knees,* and remember that it is not the number of *chapters* you read which will benefit you, but the amount of *blessing* you receive from the portion, however small, that God brings beneath your eye.

3d. To keep in touch with God a Salvation soldier should be a prevailer in prayer.

Again, it does not lie in the length, or wording, or power of the prayer, but in the *grip of God,* obtained by the faith of the one who prays. There is no reason why you should not enter into God's presence, touch His very heart, and receive in return the answer to your prayer in a minute and a half or two minutes. It is a mistake to think that only those people who have the time to spend hours on their knees every day can be considered in close touch with God. All Salvationists, however much or however little time they are able to spend alone with God, should *live always in the spirit of prayer*—"continuing instant in prayer" all day long, able to turn and open their hearts to God at any minute of the day, that, when most tempted and tried, they may ever receive just that which their souls need. Remember that prayer will ever prove your greatest help to piety.

II.—GODLINESS IN DAILY LIFE.

The natural outcome of a holy soul is a holy life, and this is the most difficult and perhaps the most trying part of a soldier's warfare. There are the home trials, an unsaved family, ever ready to ridicule or thwart anything that speaks of living religion. An irreligious and unsympathetic employer, or work-companions, sick children, loss of situation, poverty, persecution and a hundred and one other trials that stalk about like a great army of enemies trying to aim poisoned darts at a soldier's consistent, pious life. Herein lies the soldier's cross, but also his greatest power. Watch your life. A loss of temper, a discontented, grumbling disposition, a fault-finding spirit, petty jealousies, or a cowardly fear of confessing Christ would make your life a failure.

"If it be possible, as much as lieth in you, live peaceably with all men."

1st. Watch your words.—A little word spoken impatiently, an unkind reflection upon somebody else, the repeating of some little bit of empty gossip, may prove in your life the first step to inconsistency. The world has a long tongue, and worldlings are characterized by their love of talking about everything and nothing. Gossip and slander, spleen and jealousy, are day after day being poured in a great torrent from the lips of those who are thus proclaiming themselves to the world *little-souled* people. Oh, the life-long harm and heart-break and misery that empty talk has occasioned! If you don't watch your words and guard your lips, your influence as a Salvation soldier will be lost. Let it be a principle with you that one of the essentials, and most visible ones, too, to a pious life is *a consecrated mouth*, that should speak only the words that Jesus Christ Himself would speak, were He on earth. Remember the words,

" Whoso keepeth his mouth and his tongue keepeth his soul from troubles."

"I will keep my mouth with a bridle."

2d. Watch your manner.—Your heart and its feelings are hidden away from the world and your comrades beneath your exterior seeming and manner, and may unintentionally, and perhaps unknowingly, spoil their influence by a wrong or unwise action in this respect. Coldness of manner, denoted by a stiff, critical, off-hand way of dealing with others, carries the impression with it that pride and self have not yet been subjugated by God and love. Light, frivolous, giddy manners naturally make an onlooker believe that the soul lacks depth, solidity and piety, and an indifferent, uninterested, easy-going manner is a clear index of backsliding from first love and zeal in God's service. Every Salvation soldier should pray for the grace to shun and keep clear of each and every one of these appearances of evil, for they have driven many a poor, seeking sinner away from God and true religion, not being able to discern the inconsistency of such professors.

"I will take heed to my ways."

3d. Beware of self.—The most hideous,

powerful and poisonous weed in the soul's gar-
den is *self.* Its roots are something like that of
the dandelion, which grow to such a depth in the
earth that it is quite a task to unroot them, and
its seeds, we fear, are almost as innumerable and
as light as the little white-winged seeds of that
plant, which the wind scatters by thousands from
the parent-plant. Nothing will mar a Salvation soldier's usefulness so speedily and thoroughly as the prominence and importance of the
" I " in his life. Self-importance will not bring
glory to God ; self-conceit has never yet lifted
high the standard of the cross ; self-love has
never yet led a soul up Calvary's mountain.

There is not one word or action recorded in the
whole life of Christ which reflected a shadow of
selfishness, and this was one of the causes of His
wonderful power. All the way from the manger
to the cross, His entire abandonment of self-pleas-
ing, self-ease, and self-importance stands forth
clear and unquestionable, and it is easy to see
that it was this spirit that urged Him forward
through a life of suffering to a death of shame.

If a Salvationist is to succeed in impressing the world with his piety, he must cease to seek his *own*—to seek his own pleasure, to think of his own comfort, or tread the path of ease, for the follower of Jesus must of necessity walk as He walked. The Man of Sorrows gave up His home to seek the wandering sons of men; the Salvationist must be ready to do the same, should the call come. Jesus of Nazareth had no reputation and was contemptible and nowhere in the opinion of the world of His day; His followers in the nineteenth century must be willing likewise to live to please *God* and not *man*, and to have all manner of evil said about them for His sake.

"If any man will come after Me, let him deny himself, and take up his cross and follow Me."

A self-sacrificing life is the only thing that will enable a Salvationist to make an impression upon the people of America to-day. You say, "I love sinners;" the sinners answer, "*Show us your love;*" and all through, in every profession of religion you make, the world demands a practical, whole-hearted manifestation of the same.

III.—GODLINESS ON THE PLATFORM.

We cannot over-estimate the importance of our platform or public life. It is a sort of public invitation to the outside world to come and look at Christ in and through us, and, to a great extent, this is what they really come to see. Before a sinner seeks to look at Jesus for himself, he strives to see Him in the men and women who, though once like himself, have become representatives of the Saviour. If the eye of the world watches and criticises the soldier's private life, how closely must it scrutinize his action and manner on the platform! To show to the world that you are a real, whole-hearted follower of Christ, and to manifest your piety of life upon the platform, you will have to watch and check yourself constantly.

" See then that ye walk circumspectly."

Ist. Every true soldier should be a soul-speaker.—Let your speaking be the outpouring of your own soul. Do not aim at eloquence. Two of God's most useful and powerful instruments in the eyes of the world would have possessed very little of the qualifications needed by a speaker. Moses, when called by God, confessed to having a "stammering tongue," and the Apostle Paul, either for this reason or for some other, called his speech "contemptible." Yet, in both cases, the Lord filled their mouths with burning words, the power and spirit of which are felt even until this day. Eloquent men very often get swallowed up in their eloquence and *lose their spiritual power*. Be simple and NATURAL in speaking. Shun imitation in style, words, or attitude of anyone else. Just be yourself, and throw your soul in all its weakness and simplicity upon the strength and wisdom of Him alone who can fill your mind with thoughts, your lips with words, and your words with power. Do not let your speaking become a form, a repetition, of some oft-repeated sentences, but just as you are always getting something fresh to talk about in your daily life, so seek for some fresh way of carrying the old, old story into sinners' hearts. Let all you say be said in your natural voice. Oh, how

many wear out their throats and nerves, and
spoil the stirring words they speak by pitching
their voice on a very high note and screaming!
We know that this is a difficulty to many; they
are carried away with their desire to bring the
truth before the people, and often imagine that
they are not heard when speaking in their ordi-
nary voice. But remember, there is nothing more
trying to an audience than to hear speakers thus
straining themselves, and, in many instances, it
makes the words quite inaudible. *Talk naturally*, throwing all the passion and feeling and
anxiety of your soul into your words, and your
speaking shall prove to the people the reality and
godliness of your soul.

**2d. In a soldier's platform work a contin-
uous exercise of faith is necessary.** Nothing
looks worse to an audience than an uninterested,
listless manner in a soldier who is not directly
taking part in the proceedings. There must be
something radically wrong in the zeal and piety
of a soldier who only takes an interest in his or
her little part of the meeting, and, when another

is speaking, praying, or singing, sits listlessly by, reading a WAR CRY, whispering, laughing, or looking about. The exercise of continuous faith and the manifestation of real interest on your part throughout the meeting will be noticed and appreciated by the audience, whereas the reverse would be a *hindrance* and drawback to many. To see a Salvation soldier leave the hall *directly the first meeting is over*, and the prayer-meeting, which should be the most important part of the night's meeting, begins, is another hindrance to those who have just heard that very soldier, perhaps, say how anxious he was to get souls saved.

3d. Personal responsibility should be felt by every soldier on the platform. The responsibility of souls in any meeting cannot be said to rest upon the leader of that corps only. Every Salvation soldier should bear souls upon his heart, and remember that God expects each man to do his duty. Even if you do not open your lips in prayer or song or speech, you have in faith your part to do in that meeting. If you cannot speak from the platform, you can speak to individuals in the audience. If you can do nothing else, your happy face and your saved manner can speak of God's work in your own soul, and by your piety on the platform you can convince the world of the reality of your profes sion.

"Let your light so shine before men, that they may see your good works and glorify your Father which is in heaven."

PRACTICE.

I.—SOLDIERSHIP IS ONE OF THE CRYING NEEDS OF THE PRESENT AGE.

There has been plenty of preaching, talking, and praying, but none of these ever won a battle, unless backed home by a real, practical activity in the holy war. No one can question the need of soldiership in the Lord's Army. If you will study your Bibles, you will find innumerable commands, promises, and instructions, which liken the Christian life to a warfare, God's gifts to armor, and the resisting of evil to a battle.

1st. Need of the world.—A glance at the world at the present day, given over to pleasure-seeking, money-making, self-aggrandizement and the race for fame, with such utter regardlessness of God, and disregard of His commands shows us that nothing but a desperate and real attack upon sin in all its forms can be successful. We have a real enemy to face, and in the drunkard's blasted life, the pleasure-seeker's unsatisfied existence and the infidel's dark hopelessness, we can see a real, terrible and crying need, of men and women who will go forward beneath the banner to do and dare for Christ.

"The whole world lieth in wickedness."

2d. Soldiership a channel for holy energy. —When first converted, the heart of every sinner, realizing God's love to him, is kindled in return with a portion of that same love which makes him long to seek and save his fellowmen. Alas, in hundreds this precious zeal, born of God for the blessing of mankind, becomes weak, dwindles away, and at last is altogether lost. Having found no vent, with no special aim or channel in which to work, they have lost their desire of blessing others, and in consequence have lost all the vitality of their salvation. Now, if for nothing else, there is a need of soldiership to call out and keep in action this love and zeal in God's service. Nothing will keep your soul healthier than to be wholly absorbed and ever at work for *the blessing of others*. As true soldiership calls for love, devotion and bravery, backed home by the true war spirit, rather than the qualifications of education, eloquence and ability, The Army has opened a sphere of usefulness and devotion to hundreds of young men and women, who might otherwise have *wasted their lives on self*. In the breast of every true, brave man who loves his country, there dwells a spirit which, when that country is threatened by an invading army, makes him seize the sword and vents itself in battle to the death. We are not of this world, but we have a kingdom, and in the breast of every subject there should breathe a *quenchless spirit*, urging him ever onward to battle for it, against the powers of darkness which, on every hand, are crowning our King with thorns, instead of honor and glory, and crying " Crucify !" instead of " Hail Him !"   Seek the war spirit, and when you have it, never quench it by inaction.

" He * * * was clad with zeal as a cloak."

" When the enemy shall come in like a flood, the Spirit of the Lord shall lift up a standard against him."

3d.   Soldiership a bond of union.—Having

one aim, one captain, and one common interest has ever proved the main spring of unity in the world's great armies. Unity among saved souls is necessary to success, and in soldiership has been found to exist the bond of union needed. Salvation soldiers have all the same aim in view, the same interests at stake, the same persecutions to bear, the same blessed victories to rejoice over. We are all in one great Army, and being part of the Army each soldier should have an interest in it; in fact, it should be the soldier's *first* interest. If the bond is broken, and any soldier begins to think of his own interest or to *consider himself* as separate and different from his soldier comrades, it is a sure sign that the true war spirit is waning. In a killing army, such a soldier would become more a hindrance than a help, and is it not so in the Holy Army? SEPARATE INTERESTS MEAN DIVISION AND DIVISION MEANS DEFEAT.

"Now the God of patience and consolation grant you to be like-minded one toward another according to Christ Jesus :

"That ye may with one mind *and* one mouth

glorify God, even the Father of our Lord Jesus Christ."—Romans xv. 5 and 6.

II.—REALITY OF SOLDIERSHIP.

The critical and *uninformed* world, which knows nothing of God's warfare, but what it casually sees and hears by chance is very apt to say that we are merely *playing at soldiers*, and we are often looked at with a sort of pitying, patronizing forbearance by men and women who, in *all their lives*, have never passed through such real and desperate fighting as we encounter in one week. It is a real war which must be embraced with as much determination, and faced with as much courage as any earthly battlefield requires. It calls for even greater sacrifice and keener suffering. Their suffering and sacrifice principally affects the *body*, ours, the soul, with all its keen affections and sensitive feelings. An earthly war lasts but a certain time, with battles scattered through it at intervals, and some who join the army are never called to face the cannon or the bayonet; whereas, our warfare lasts the *lifetime*, with daily, hourly battles, and every soldier has his place to fill. Are you a *real* soldier? in spirit, in *courage*, in determination, in *endurance?* one who is as brave when surrounded by enemies as in the midst of comrades and friends? one never ashamed to confess Christ and willing to stand *alone* for Him at all costs, though it mean the sacrifice of home, and dear ones, love ease, wealth and even *life?* If so, you can have the joy of feeling that your life shall convince the world of the true soldiership of a follower of the cross. It means something to put your name to the following Articles of War, and surely none but a true soldier can live up to them.

"For, behold, I have made thee this day a defenced city, and an iron pillar, and brazen walls against the whole land.

"And they shall fight against thee: but they shall not prevail against thee; for I *am* with thee, saith the Lord, to deliver thee."

"Before the name of any person is entered on the Roll, his experience and conversation must give evidence—

" That he is saved from the guilt and power of sin, through true repentance and faith in the blood of Christ."

" That he is a total abstainer from all intoxicating drinks, from cursing and swearing and from lying and fraud of every kind."

" That he is acting justly and honestly towards his own family and neighbors, and those with whom he works or does business."

" That he is willing to obey the orders of his superior officers in all matters relating to the Salvation War."

" That he will be true in every way to the interests of The Army, regular in attending its meetings, outside and in, as often as he can."

" That he will, as far as possible, take part in all its works, give to its funds, make known its publications and defend it from injury."

ARTICLES OF WAR.

1st.—Having received with all my heart the salvation offered to me by the tender mercy of

Jehovah, I do here and now publicly acknow-
ledge God to be my Father and King, Jesus
Christ to be my Saviour, and the Holy Spirit
to be my guide, comforter and strength;
and that I will, by His help, love, serve, worship,
and obey this glorious God through all time and
through all eternity.

2d.—Believing solemnly that The Salvation
Army has been created by God, and is sustained
and directed by Him, I do here declare my full
determination, by God's help, to be a true soldier
of The Army till I die.

3d.—I do here, and now, and forever, renounce
the world with all its sinful pleasures, compan-
ionships, treasures, and objects, and declare my
full determination boldly to show myself a soldier of Jesus Christ in all places and companies,
no matter what I may have to suffer, do, or lose,
by so doing.

4th.—I do here and now declare that I will abstain from the use of all intoxicating liquors and
also from the habitual use of opium, laudanum,
morphia, and all other baneful drugs except

when in illness such drugs shall be ordered for me by a doctor.

5th.—I do here and now declare that I will abstain from the use of all low or profane language; from the taking of the name of God in vain; and from taking part in any unclean conversation or the reading of any obscene book or paper at any time, in any company, or in any place.

6th.—I do here declare that I will not allow myself in any falsehood, deceitfulness, misrepresentation or dishonesty; neither will I practise any fraudulent conduct, either in my business, my home, or in any other relation in which I may stand to my fellowmen, but that I will deal truthfully, fairly, honorably and kindly with all those who may employ me, or whom I may myself employ.

7th.—I do here declare that I will never treat any woman, child or other person, whose life, comfort or happiness may be placed within my power, in an oppressive, cruel, or cowardly manner, but that I will protect such from evil and danger so far as I can, and promote, to the utmost of my ability, their present welfare and eternal salvation.

8th.—I do here declare that I will spend all the time, strength, money and influence I can in supporting and carrying on this war, and that I will endeavor to lead my family, friends, neighbors, and all others whom I can influence, to do the same, believing that the sure and only way to remedy all the evils in the world is by bringing men to submit themselves to the government of the Lord Jesus Christ.

9th.—I do here declare that I will always obey the lawful orders of my officers, and that I will carry out to the utmost of my power all the Orders and Regulations of the Army; and further, that I will be an example of faithfulness to its principles, advance to the utmost of my ability its operations, and never allow, where I can prevent it, any injury to its interests or hindrance to its success.

10th.—And I do here and now call upon all present to witness that I enter into this undertaking of my own free will, feeling that the love of Christ who died to save me requires from me this devotion of my life to His service for the salvation of the whole world.

III.—SIGNS OF SOLDIERSHIP.

It would be of very little use for the soldiers of an earthly army to be soldiers in heart, spirit or talk only. Outward, visible signs of their calling are not only necessary, but are always a condition of soldiership. We have sometimes pictured to our ourselves the utter confusion and disaster which would be the sure conse- quence of two opposing armies meeting on the battlefield, with no *distinctive uniform* in their ranks, but every man wearing just what he chose. As a natural consequence, fellow-country- men would be mistaking each other for enemies and shooting the very men they should have protected, whereas the enemy might often escape without harm.   Uniform to them is a necessity, and the man who is ashamed of the uniform of his country is considered a coward, a traitor and a *deserter.*

If *we* are real soldiers why should we be ashamed to wear the distinctive uniform of our Army? If *not*, how can we be outwardly known when passing among worldlings, as being in the world, but not of it?

1st.—The primary advantage and benefit of uniform is to enable us to literally obey the Lord's commands to come out from among the world and be separate.

What have we to do with the silly, tawdry, worldly fashions of the godless? Ought not our minds to be free from the constant worry and anxiety that worldlings experience in keeping pace with fashion, and ought we not to discard the very appearance of vanity and pride which worldly dress denotes? We do not believe that the wearing of jewelry, feathers, flowers, or any other such ornament is compatible with the blessing of a clean heart, and we are certain that no one thus dressed can with a clear conscience and the certainty of success preach the following of the Man of Sorrows, whose life was one of sacrifice and pure, wholehearted devotion.

" Wherefore come out from among them, and be ye separate, saith the Lord, and touch not the unclean thing; and I will receive you."

" In like manner also, that women adorn themselves in modest apparel. . . with *sobriety;* not with braided hair, or gold, or pearls, or costly array."

2d.—The uniform is unquestionably a great help to every soldier in remaining faithful and resisting temptation from the world.

For instance, a soldier who had formerly been a chronic drunkard might be fiercely pressed by his soul's enemy to slip into a saloon and take again the accursed drink, but with the S's on his collar, and Army band on his cap he would instinctively say to himself, "I can never enter there in uniform," and this *safeguard* might go a long way in helping him to resist in this hour of weakness his soul's tempter. The uniform keeps converts *clear from harmful companionship;* for there is never communion between light and darkness, so the worldly, giddy, godless crowd keep clear of the man or woman whose dress denotes that they are separate from them.

" Whosoever therefore will be the friend of the world is the enemy of God."

" And ye shall be holy unto me: for I the Lord am holy, and have severed you from other people, that ye should be mine."

3d.—Remember that uniform is a wonderful testimony for Jesus Christ.

The blue dress and Army bonnet, red guernsey and soldier's cap, with the S's and shields, speak to everyone, whose eye may fall upon them, of *salvation.*   Even where it is impossible to speak a word for God, the uniform thus speaks, and in many instances just opens the way to deal with people concerning their souls.   It also manifests to the world that even in this day of sham, infidelity and worldliness there is a people sufficiently in earnest about the religion that they profess not to be ashamed to wear a distinctive dress in testimony of their faith.

" Whosoever shall confess Me before men, him shall the Son of Man also confess before the angels of God."

" Ye are the light of the world."

" Let your light so shine before men that they may see your good works, and glorify your Father which is in heaven."

4th.—The uniform, when anyway possible, should be worn all day long, and not only in meetings and parades or on Sundays. It is just possible that your daily work is such that a uniform would be spoiled were you to wear it. In such case you would be quite justified in only wearing the shield and S's ; but no soldier, on any consideration, should wear at any time *worldly, gaudy apparel.* All that is artificial and false should be avoided. Uniform should be worn out of *principle,* because it is right and God-pleasing and helpful in The Army warfare, and not alone because it is an Army regulation. Do not be ashamed to show your colors, any more than politicians or earthly soldiers are ashamed of theirs. Wear it for the honor of God.

" Whether therefore ye eat, or drink, or whatsoever ye do, do all to the glory of God."

IV.—OFFICES OF SOLDIERSHIP.

1st.—Helping the officer.—Sometimes the idea exists that the commanding officer of the corps is to be the whole and sole responsible party in it; that all the work, whether outdoor or indoor, and the many extra duties which arise in connection therewith, are to be arranged and accomplished by *him alone*, and that no one else need take any responsible part in the warfare. This idea is altogether erroneous. Soldiers should remember that *they*, as well as the officers, are The Salvation Army, and that it is absolutely necessary for the welfare of the whole, that each individual should fill his respective office and do his very utmost to help his commanding officer who has been sent to lead The Army forward. This can be done in many ways, a few of which we will mention. A soldier's first duty is

(*a.*) Ready and cheerful obedience.

It is impossible to organize an army unless the soldiers of the same are willing to follow the leadings and guidings of their leader, and just as all officers are expected to obey their general, so it is necessary for all soldiers to obey their officers. The question may arise, "Is this not a despotic rule?" to which we answer "No!" Every Salvationist enters the ranks understanding thoroughly what is expected of him, and places himself willingly and cheerfully beneath the guidance of his officers, precisely the same as the children of Israel did beneath Moses, Joshua and Gideon whom they accepted as their leaders led of God, and no one who is not inspired with this spirit need stay in The Salvation Army an hour longer than he chooses. Of course, where there does not exist in the hearts of soldiers the spirit of willingness and determination to do their utmost for the advancement of the war, obedience will cease to become a *pleasure* and will prove a *task*. It is well to remember that our willingness to obey can be used by us as a test of the growth of devotion or selfishness in our souls.

"And they answered Joshua, saying, All thou commandest us we will do, and whithersoever thou sendest, we will go. According as we hearkened unto Moses in all things, so will we hearken unto thee."

" By love serve one another."

(*b.*) Open-air work.

One of the soldier's most useful offices and grandest opportunities can be found in the open-air. The testimony, song and prayers uttered in the streets of our crowded cities reach the ear of thousands who would otherwise never be reached and warned. A faithful soldier will love the open-air field, and be present in foul weather as well as fine, in cold as well as heat; in fact, should consider it his *duty* to be present if possible whenever the officer takes his stand in the streets.

" Go out quickly into the streets and lanes of the city, and bring in hither the poor, and the maimed, and the halt and the blind."

" Go out into the highways and hedges, and compel them to come in, that My house may be filled."

(*c.*) "War Cry" selling.

The duty of pushing, announcing, and disposing of the WAR CRYS is often left entirely with the officer, as if it was their concern alone and did not affect the corps. The WAR CRY is *every soldier's paper*, and if each soldier took upon himself the responsibility of making this paper a success and exercised a real interest in it, what a vast amount of good this salvation journal would accomplish. Surely every soldier ought to be responsible for the sale of a dozen, or at least half-a-dozen WAR CRYS every week, and as the WAR CRY has been instrumental in saving so many and in blessing thousands already, who knows how much more good might be accomplished as the result of this extra effort. There are numberless ways in which the WAR CRY can be sold.

1.—Soldiers could sell the WAR CRY on the streets, and though unsuccessful with some people, yet would sell the paper to others.

2.—Soldiers should ask the captain to form them into WAR CRY Brigades, and to advise them in the art of selling them.

3.—Soldiers should themselves become responsible for taking and disposing of a certain number weekly.

4.—Soldiers should themselves report on the meetings in their corps for the CRY, and are invited to compose songs and write interesting portions of their lives or any startling incidents which may come under their notice.

5.—Soldiers could keep a few in their store and circulate them among their workmates.

6.—Above all soldiers should *read the* WAR CRY *themselves,* and we are sure this will prove the chief incentive to their effort in its sale. They will find endless matter to talk about, publicly, besides understanding better the movement to which they belong.

" Be instant in season and out of season."

" Whatsoever thy hand findeth to do, do it with all thy might."

(*d.*) Dealing with souls.

It is impossible for the captain of any corps to undertake alone the dealing with souls in an after-meeting or at the penitent-form. Every soldier should consider this one of their special privileges, and this important service needs much care and wisdom and patience. A sinner at the penitent-form should always be made first to see the vital importance of the step taken; secondly, the unworthiness, wickedness and meanness of a sinful and selfish life, lived so long regardless of God, His claims and His mercy; thirdly, the necessity of thorough, *whole-hearted repentance* should be made very clear, so that they shall not fall into the error of thinking that faith is the only requisite before obtaining salvation. Remember God's unalterable condition of pardon is the forsaking of evil. Fourthly, a penitent should be allowed *to deal with God himself* and left alone to pray, and not talked to unceasingly at the penitent-form, for it is God alone who can save, and continuous talking to a soul while forward may prove more a hindrance than a help. Above all, it is necessary for a soldier who would be a successful soul-winner to have his heart full of *tender love* and *compassion for the sinner.* It is only thus equipped that he can ever be successful.   Be a *soul-lover* and a *soul-winner*.

"They that turn many to righteousness shall shine as the stars for ever and ever."

(*e.*) **Loyalty.**

Nothing is more absolutely necessary in a soldier's warfare than a thorough possession and exhibition of loyalty.   A loyal soldier will not allow anything damaging to be said about his officer; a loyal soldier will always check, and, if he fails in this, report any talk or inference or actions that may be damaging to The Army or its leaders.   A soldier possessed with this spirit will be loyal and true to our General and his representative, and any officer in command over him, independent of personal likes and dis- likes, as long as that officer on his side be loyal and true to the spirit and principles of The Salvation Army.   A soldier should beware of becoming absorbed and carried away exclusively with the in- terests of his own corps.   They should remember the interests of the whole great movement; that their little corps is but a tiny corner of the great battlefield.   This spirit manifests itself thus, *they* must always have a first-grade officer; all the specials must visit them; but every collection must go to their barracks, their brass band, or some other local interest; Headquarters must always answer their letters and attend to their trade orders, never mind how many other corps may be waiting, and woe be to the poor Marshal or his representative if he does not send along the officer for whom they petition, or leave in the corps the one whose term they wish to have extended. *God banish this spirit from every soldier and corps.* The Army is a great, glorious whole, and each part should minister to its well-being, while every soldier should remember that they have the interest not only of one town to consider at Headquarters, but the well being and advancement of the precious cause in hundreds of other cities and towns, and a truly loyal soldier will always bear this fact in mind.

"Be thou faithful unto death, and I will give thee a crown of life."

"Thou hast been faithful over a few things; I will make thee ruler over many things."

2d.—Helping fellow-comrades.—The greatest
strength of any Salvation Army corps is unity,
and the only hope of unity is the spirit of love
and forbearance. There are a thousand little
ways in which soldiers can either help or hinder
each other in the warfare. How many there are
in every corps who are weak and need the helping hand of one stronger in faith and courage, and
there is nothing more sad than to feel that in the
way of such should be put a stumbling-block by
the very men and women who should be the most
eager to help them forward

"Bear ye one another's burdens, and so fulfil
the law of Christ."

**(*a*.) The past of a soldier should never be
brought up against him by a comrade.**

One of the *cruellest* hindrances that can be
thrown in the way of one who has turned from
a life of sin is being constantly reminded of his
past, or hearing it brought up in gossip. If a
man was a thief, why let the memory of his sin
hang about him in suspicion or condemnation,
when striving to be an honest man? If a woman

did once tread a path of dishonor, why brand her
with the stain of shame forever, when Jesus has
forgiven her and sent her on her way, cleansed
in His most precious blood, to sin no more? If
a soldier, even after conversion, should slip and
return again repentant, how hard that his future
life shall always have this one slip brought up
against it, when Jesus Christ said to Peter that
his brother should be forgiven, not seven times,
but seventy times seven. We are pretty sure
he meant not only forgiven, but forgotten. When
Jesus Christ pardons a sinner He washes away
and blots out his sins. Every true soldier should
sacredly guard any knowledge of a fellow-soldier
which might hinder that one, unless it be any
known sin or fault which should be reported to
the captain, or mentioned to them personally in
all love.

"Why dost thou set at naught thy brother?
For we shall all stand before the judgment seat
of Christ."

"As far as the East is from the West, so far
hath He removed our transgressions from us."

(*b.*) **A comrade's peculiarities should never be ridiculed.**

No two natures are alike. God has moulded every heart, every being, every body differently. Some are intensely sensitive, while others seem sometimes indifferent to feeling altogether. A slight peculiarity of manner, speech, voice, or deformity of body is in no way a fault, and it is both cruel and mean to ridicule those who display such. Mistakes can be made by all of us; how unjustifiable, then, to make fun at the expense of one who has committed an error. Those who are very sensitive can sometimes be more tortured by ridicule than they would be by the scorching of their flesh in an inquisition chamber; and surely, every Salvationist has enough ridicule to stand from the world, without having to encounter it among those who should uphold, encourage and comfort him.

"He that is void of wisdom despiseth his neighbor: but a man of understanding holdeth his peace."

"The heart knoweth its own bitterness, and a stranger doth not meddle therewith."

(c.) Strengthening the weak should be the duty of the strong.

It should always be remembered that many of those who come out to our penitent-form have been saved from lives of sin and degradation that makes their early days on the right road a series of bitter and testing temptations. A drunkard's feet cannot be expected to tread the path as firmly and determinedly from the onset as when he becomes strong and steady in his Christian life, but how wonderfully he might be helped by the firm, loving hand of a comrade, and a cheering word of welcome, making him feel that others cared about him. The more experience soldiers have, the more responsible they are held by God in the cheering, blessing, and strengthening, of those who have not been as long saved as themselves. The point is not, to show the weak one how weak he is, and make him painfully feel by contrast how strong and advanced you are in growth, but to take him right up to Jesus, the Source of strength, inspire him with hope, and cheer him with encouragement, which will do more to strengthen his spiritual life than anything you can do

In summing up the duty and service required from every faithful Salvationist, can we not do so in the sentence so oft repeated, which if as fully practiced, would make of every professor a practical soldier, "Not my will, but the will of my Father;" or, "Thy will be done." Let us take for our copy nothing less than the life of Jesus Christ. Let us seek to walk on no other path than the one dyed by His own blood, and let us ask no greater honor than to share His cross, and help Him in His life-work of seeking the lost, living, as He did, a life of self-sacrifice, and always putting the kingdom and its interests first and foremost in our lives. If we live thus, we shall die thus, and triumphantly pass from death unto life to hear Him say,

" Well done thou good and faithful servant, enter thou into the joy of thy Lord."

GENERAL COVENANTS.

V.—COVENANT SERVICE.

Oh, thou Everlasting God, my Father and my Friend, I have come before Thee, I am in Thy presence, I am at Thy feet. Thou seest me, and just here and now I desire with all my heart to make a covenant with Thee, that shall never be broken.

Thou hast loved me with an everlasting love, knowing all my sinfulness, rebellion, and unfaithfulness. Thou didst give Thy Son Jesus Christ to die for me on Mount Calvary, in order that my sins might be forgiven me, and an entrance might be opened for me into the kingdom of heaven.

When I wandered in ignorance and sin Thou didst seek me, and win me to Thyself by Thy Spirit, and when I came to Thee, tortured with guilt and burdened with sin, Thou didst remove far from me the curse and penalty I had justly deserved, and didst cleanse my heart in the precious blood of Thy Son, and give me power over the world, the flesh, and the devil. And since that time Thou hast kept me by Thy power, supplied my need, conquered my enemies, and bestowed upon me indescribable and unnumbered mercies ; and, through the merits of Thy love and death, I come again into Thy presence, entering into the holiest place by Thine own invitation, and make this covenant with Thee.

In so doing, I take Thee again to be my God and my Saviour, and promise to worship, to obey, and to serve Thee with all my heart, with all my soul, with all my mind, and with all my strength.

I rely upon Thee to supply all my need, to assist me in all my conflicts with the powers of evil, and to bring me off more than conqueror over earth and hell, and I trust Thee, my Saviour, whose precious blood does just now cleanse me from all unrighteousness, to keep me clean and present me faultless in the presence of Thy Father at the last great judgment day.

Blessed Jesus, the world despises Thee, but I glory in Thee; the world hates Thee, but I love Thee; for Thy sake I separate myself from the world, from its amusements, from its friendships, from its fashions, and from its aims ; and I now promise that I will follow Thee with all my heart, obey Thee with all my strength, cleave to Thee with all my affection, and fight for Thee all my days.

Here now, in the presence of my comrades, deliberately and forever, I give Thee my body, that it may be a temple of the Holy Ghost ; my life, that it may be lived ceaselessly doing Thy will in bringing blessings to those around me; my pos-sessions, that they may be unselfishly held for the good of Thy kingdom; and my heart, that it may love only what is good, true, benevolent, and beautiful in Thy sight, and be Thy own everlasting dwelling-place.

All I have, and all I hope to be, I lay upon Thy altar for joy or for sorrow, for prosperity or adversity, asking only that I may have the high privilege of sharing with Thee the sufferings of Thy Christ, and the honor of bringing glory to Thy name, and salvation to the precious souls for whom Thou didst shed Thy blood.

And now, O God the Father, God the Son, and God the Holy Ghost, Thou great Jehovah, for evermore I belong to Thee; Thou art my God, and I am Thy child, Thy servant, and Thy soldier. To Thee I look for strength to enable me to fulfil these solemn promises, and to seal by Thine Almighty Spirit, through the precious blood of Jesus Christ, this covenant which I have made, and to grant unto me that wisdom and strength which will enable me to keep these sacred vows even unto death, and so may the promises I make on earth be ratified in heaven *Amen!*

VI.—WAR COVENANT.

In view of the wicked and wretched condition of the men and women around us, and the danger to which they are every hour exposed, of being lost for ever in hell, and assured of the possibility of their being rescued from sin and misery by the power of God through Jesus Christ, as proved by the experience of so many Salvation soldiers in various places, I desire here and now for the glory of God and the salvation of souls, to give myself, with all I possess, with all my heart, afresh and forever, to the Salvation war.

In doing this I now pledge myself before God, before my dear Saviour who died for me, and before my comrades, to use what time, talent, means, and influence I possess to advance the interests of the war in my own corps, or neighborhood, or wherever I may go.

In carrying out this covenant I promise to accept of any position, do any work, or fulfil any commission that may be given me by my officers according to the orders and regulations of The Army.

I promise to sing, pray, engage in any other duty, or occupy any post required from me in any meeting, whether it be held indoors or in the open air.

I promise to give all the leisure time I can to the war, to attend knee-drill, to be punctual at the commencement of every service, to stay to the end of the prayer-meetings, and to be diligent in attending and working in all other meetings, so far as I possibly can.

I promise to wear uniforms, sell " WAR CRYS," engage in such visitation as I may be directed, and to strive to make myself in every way a thoroughly efficient soldier.

I here promise to pray for my comrades both far and near at all convenient times ; but espe cially at 12.30 p.m., and after meals daily.   At these times I will pray particularly for those who are in circumstances of persecution, poverty, or peril.

I will try to give every satisfaction to my em- ployers or to those with whom I live and work, so as to commend The Army in the eyes of the ungodly.

If called upon to do so, I will go out as an officer, giving up my life entirely to the work of saving souls, and will go to any country or labor for the salvation of any class for which I may be thought best adapted.

In general, I here promise God that I will at all times obey Him, daily seeking light, and power at His hands, and walking in that light, by that power, whatever cost or trouble, suffering or difficulty, it may involve, and ask God my Father, for Jesus Christ's sake, to give me strength faithfully to carry out these resolutions. *Amen !*

WE SHALL WIN AMERICA.

BY BALLINGTON BOOTH.

We shall win America for our heavenly King;
Hear its dying millions of salvation sing,
   Washed in the blood of the Lamb.
We will plant our colors in every state and clime,
Loudest hallelujahs from all our soldiers chime—
   Washed in the blood of the Lamb.

CHORUS.

   We shall win America over to our King;
   Hear its dying millions of salvation sing.
   Hurrah! Hurrah! The day of victory's nigh.
   Fight on! Fight on! We'll conquer or we'll die.

Though clouds of opposition o'er our sky be cast,
Yet every vale of shadows with Jesus shall be past,
   Trusting in the strength of the King.
The chaffing and the laughing – aye, all the world may do,
Cannot mar the victory the Lord will bring us through —
   Trusting in the strength of the King.

We'll raise a host of praying men with Daniel's courage bold;
In our ranks brave girls shall march, as Miriam did of old,
   Led by the arm of the Lord.
Courageous as was Joshua, we'll cross each swelling flood,
And intercede like Esther for the people of our God -
   Led by the arm of the Lord.

Far braver than the bravest of earthly volunteers
Are the true Salvationists, who through the scoffs and jeers
   Live for the Kingdom of the Lord.
Soon with gathering warriors in council round the throne
We'll stand confessed by Jesus, triumphant as His own—
   Forever in the presence of the Lord.

SALVATION ARMY AUXILIARY LEAGUE.

———o———

WHAT IS THE AUXILIARY LEAGUE?

The Auxiliary League is composed of those persons who, while not obliged to endorse and approve every single method used by The Army, are sufficiently in sympathy with the great work of reclaiming drunkards, rescuing the fallen, and saving the lost, as to give it their prayer, influence and money.

Subscribers are asked to contribute *Five Dollars* per annum , are supplied every year, on payment of their subscription, with a small, handsome leather ticket, bearing the official recognition of Headquarters, together with their name and number, which admits them to the meetings of the League, held periodically in various parts of the country, and ensures for them a hearty welcome in Army circles at home and abroad.

A small, neat badge bearing The Army's crest is sent to each member of the League, which, if so inclined, they can wear to denote their membership.

A copy of the *War Cry* will be mailed free to each member, weekly, after payment of subscription.

We confidently look to Auxiliaries to show their sympathy and help.

1. *By praying for us,* and especially joining our comrades throughout the States at 12.30 every day, when the soldiers of The Salvation Army, at home and abroad, pray for one another and the salvation of the world

2. *By using their influence ;* letting it be known in their own circle that they believe in us ; occasionally, at least, attending our meetings ; defending us against the numerous misrepresentations and slanders invented by enemies, and often believed and circulated by the misinformed, who frequently only need to know the real facts to come over to our side. Auxiliaries can always have the fullest information as to the truth or otherwise of any specific charge brought, *if they will write to Headquarters.*

3. *By gifts ;* assisting us in supplying funds for the current work and the constant fresh opportunities which we are constrained to seize, at home and abroad, for spreading salvation.

BALLINGTON BOOTH,
Marshal.

PUBLICATIONS

—— OF ——

THE SALVATION ARMY.

PRICE LIST:

BY THE GENERAL.

Field Officers' Orders and Regulations, postpaid, cloth $1 50
Field Officers' Orders and Regulations, to Officers (Doctrines
    and Disciplines not published separately, but included in
    the above) cloth 1 35
The Training of Children, limp, cl. 40 ; cl. boards, red edges.. 75
Salvation Soldiery, cl. 30:...... ....paper . 25
The General's Letters, cl. 60;............. .... paper.. 35
The Salvation Soldier's Guide, limp cl. 25. (Being a Bible
    chapter for morning and evening, with fragments for
    midday reading, for every day in the year) red cl. 40; red
    French morocco gilt, 75; circuit edges.. . ... 1 00

BY MRS. BOOTH.

Popular Christianity,..................................... cl..$ 75
Aggressive Christianity, cl. 50; ....p.. 25
Life and Death, cl. 50; ....p . 25
Godliness, cl. 50 ;.............................. ....p.. 35
Practical Religion, cl. 50; ....p.. 35
Church and State (in relation to The Salvation Army)..........

BY COMMISSIONER RAILTON.

Twenty-One Years' Salvation Army, cl. 50; ....p $ 35
Heathen England and The Salvation Army cl. 50; board ഗ.... 35
The Salvation Navvy (Life of Captain John Allen) cl. 50; p.. 25
Captain Ted, (Life of Capt. Edward Irons) cl. 30; ....p . 10

MISCELLANEOUS BOOKS.

Holiness Readings, 200.pages by the General, Mrs. Booth, the
    Chief-of-Staff, Miss Booth and others ....paper $ 35
House Top Saints, cl. 35 ; ....p.. 15
Life of Chas. G. Finney, (new revised edition) cl. 50;......p.. 25
Drum Taps, by E. R. S. 50; ....p.. 25
Called Out by Mr. H. and Miss E. Booth,.................cl 35
All Sides of It, ... p 15
The Salvation Soldier's Secret Drill, Thomas A. Kempis's imi-
    tation of Christ cl. 40; ....p.. 25
A Way to the World.... . ... p.. 15
A Cradle of Empire (All about the Training Home).......p . '5
Life of Capt. John O'Brine, The Seal....... ....p.. 10
Hints to Officers, 5c; per hundred 3 00
Holy Living, 5c.; per hundred 3 00
How to exalt the Masses, 5c.; per hundred.... .... 3 00
His Wrath and New Life, 5c.; per hundred 3 00
True and False Faith, ₅c.; per hundred 3 00
Dealing with Anxious Souls, 5c.; per hundred.. .... 3 00
Mercy and Judgment, 5c.; per hundred. 3 00
Save Thyself, 5c.; per hundred........................... .... 3 00
Make up Your Mind, 5c ; per hundred...................... 3 00
I Don't Care, 5c.; per hundred....................... .... 3 00
Sowing and Reaping, 5c.; per hundred................... .... 3 00
The Prodigal, or Need of Atonement, 5c.; per hundred........ 3 00
The Saved Clergyman, (John Wesley), ₅c.; per hundred...... 3 00
George Fox and The Salvation Army 200 Years Ago, 5c.; per
    hundred 3 00
A Presbyterian Salvationist (Life of Finney), 5c.; per hundred 3 00

SONGS AND MUSIC.

Salvation Army Music, vol. 1, International, 533 pieces, cloth.$0 75
Salvation Army Music, vol. 2, International, 102 pieces, cloth. 40
Salvation Army Music, vol. 1, American; mostly new pieces,
    cloth, 40c.; paper 25
Salvation Songs. 204 songs, words only, the new Song Book
    used all through America. 5
Salvation Songster, words and music, air only, paper......... 15
What to Sing, book of choruses,... 10
Songs of the Speaking, Praying and Singing Brigade; 54 pieces
    with music, paper..................................... 35

THE WAR ✶ CRY,

*THE OFFICIAL GAZETTE OF THE SALVATION
ARMY IN AMERICA,*

Consisting of sixteen pages, sixty-four columns, with illustrations, and contains the latest intelligence of the progress of Salvation Army work in all parts of the world. Also contributions from the leaders of The Army; stories of wonderful conversions; original salvation songs; lives of prominent Salvation Officers, with portraits.

Price per single copy, **5** *cts.*   *Yearly Subscription,* **$1.75.**

NEWSPAPERS AND JOURNALS.

The WAR CRY (American) wkly, 5; .... yrly, $1 75
"   "   (English) wk. 5; .... yr, .. 2)0
-"   "   (Canadian) wk. 5; .... yr, . 2 00
"   "   (California) bi-monthly 5; .... yr, .. 1 00
En Evant (French) wk. 5; ....yr, .. 2 00
Strids Ropet (Swedish) wk. 5; .... yr, .. 2 00
Der Kriegsruf (German) bi-mly, per copy 5; .... yr,   1 00
Der Heilsruf (German) wk. 5; .... yr, .. ——
"All the World ' (a monthly magazine, 36 pages,) per copy,
      10 c.; ....yr,   1 00

·

www.ingramcontent.com/pod-product-compliance
Lightning Source LLC
Chambersburg PA
CBHW032032090426
42733CB00031B/727